UPDATED EDITION

Guess What!

Workbook 3
with Digital Pack

T0343909

American English

Lynne Marie Robertson

Series Editor: Lesley Koustaff

Shaftesbury Road, Cambridge CB2 8EA, United Kingdom

One Liberty Plaza, 20th Floor, New York, NY 10006, USA

477 Williamstown Road, Port Melbourne, VIC 3207, Australia

314–321, 3rd Floor, Plot 3, Splendor Forum, Jasola District Centre, New Delhi – 110025, India

103 Penang Road, #05–06/07, Visioncrest Commercial, Singapore 238467

Cambridge University Press & Assessment is a department of the University of Cambridge.

We share the University's mission to contribute to society through the pursuit of education, learning and research at the highest international levels of excellence.

www.cambridge.org
Information on this title: www.cambridge.org/9781009798747

First published 2016
Updated edition 2024

20 19 18 17 16 15 14 13 12 11 10 9 8 7 6 5 4 3

Printed in Poland by Opolgraf

A catalogue record for this publication is available from the British Library

ISBN 978-1-009-79874-7 Workbook with Digital Pack Level 3
ISBN 978-1-009-79859-4 Student's Book with eBook Level 3
ISBN 978-1-009-79904-1 Teacher's Book with Digital Pack Level 3
ISBN 978-1-107-52807- 9 Flashcards Level 3

Additional resources for this publication at www.cambridge.org/guesswhatue

Contents

Welcome

1 **Look and write the names.**

Anna   Lily   ~~Lucas~~   Max   Tom

1   _Lucas_
2   _____
3   _____
4   _____
5   _____

2 **Look at activity 1. Read and write *true* or *false*.**

1   Tom likes art.   _true_

2   Anna is ten.   _____

3   Max is Lucas's dog.   _____

4   Lily's favorite sport is soccer.   _____

5   Lucas's favorite color is red.   _____

My picture dictionary → **Go to page 84: Find and write the new words.**

3 **Read and match.**

1 What's your name? ←
2 How old are you?
3 What's your favorite color?
4 Do you like dogs?
5 Do you have a bike?
6 Can you ride a horse?

a I'm nine years old.
b My favorite color is green.
c My name's Bill.
d Yes, I can.
e Yes, I do.
f No, I don't.

4 **Answer the questions. Then draw your picture.**

1 What's your name?

My name is _____

2 How old are you?

_____

3 Do you have a bike?

_____

4 What's your favorite color?

_____

5 Do you like dogs?

_____

6 Can you play tennis?

_____

5 Write the months in order. Then answer the question.
Use the letters in the boxes to complete the answer.

① January

② F [ ] _ _ _ _ _

③ M _ _ _ _ _

④ A _ _ _ _ _

⑤ M _ _

⑥ J _ _ [ ]

⑦ J _ [ ] _

⑧ A _ _ _ _ _

⑨ S _ _ _ _ _ _ _

⑩ O _ [ ] _ _ _ _ _

⑪ N _ [ ] _ _ _ _

⑫ D _ _ _ _ _ _ _

How many months are there?

_ W _ _ _ _

6 (About Me) **Answer the questions.**

1 What month is it?

It is _____

2 What's your favorite month?

_____

My picture dictionary → Go to page 84: Find and write the new words.

Skills: *Writing*

7 Read the email. Circle the answers to the questions.

Hello!
My name's Jill. I'm (eleven) years old. My birthday is in April.
I have one brother and one sister. I have a pet rabbit.
My favorite sport is basketball. What about you?
Jill ☺

1 How old are you?
2 When is your birthday?
3 Do you have any brothers or sisters?
4 Do you have a pet?
5 What's your favorite sport?

8 (About Me) Look at activity 7. Answer the questions for you.

1 *I'm* _____
2 _____
3 _____
4 _____
5 _____

9 (About Me) Write an email to a pen pal.

Hello! _____
My name's _____
_____
_____
_____
_____

10 (About Me) Ask and answer with a friend.

How old are you?   I'm eleven years old.

11 Read and number in order.

a — Let's do the treasure hunt together! / Good idea.

b — Treasure Hunt. Find 7 things in 7 days. Text 123 to join. A surprise at the end!

c — It's a cell phone! / And look at this!

d — Happy birthday, Lily! / Thanks, Tom. Thanks everyone for your presents! / 1

e — What's this present? / I don't know. / Open it, Lily!

f — Dad, can we do this treasure hunt, please? / Yes, of course! It sounds fun. / 123 – there!

12 Look at activity 11. Write *yes* or *no*.

1 It's Tom's birthday.   *no*

2 The present is a cell phone. _____

3 The treasure hunt is to find 7 things in 5 days. _____

4 Lily's friends don't want to do the treasure hunt. _____

5 The treasure hunt sounds fun. _____

13 **Read and check the sentences that show the value: work together.**

1 Let's do the treasure hunt together. ✓   2 Let's find my dog. ☐

3 I like card games. ☐   4 Good idea. ☐

5 Let's clean up. ☐   6 I'm playing basketball. ☐

14 **Circle the words that sound like *snake*.**

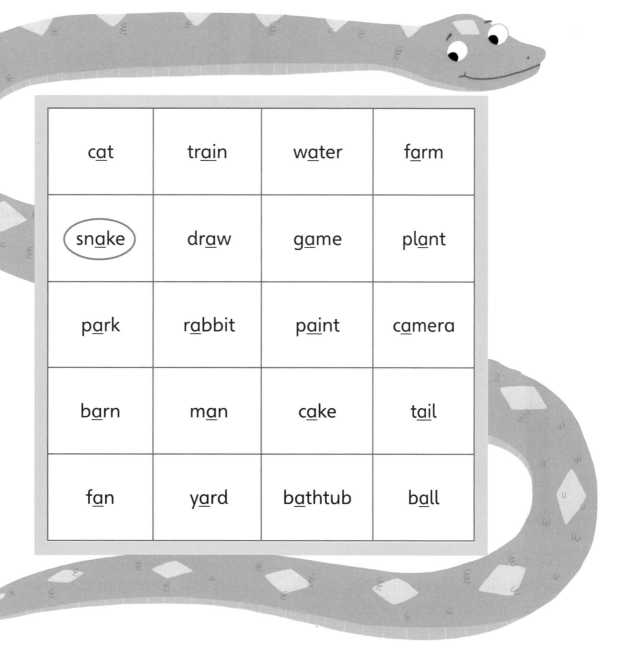

cat	train	water	farm
(snake)	draw	game	plant
park	rabbit	paint	camera
barn	man	cake	tail
fan	yard	bathtub	ball

What can you see in a landscape painting?

1 **Look and match.**

(birds)   (boat)   (forest)   (mountain)

(plants)   (river)   (ocean)   (waterfall)

2 **Draw two landscapes.**

Draw a river.
Draw some trees behind it.
Draw a boat and three ducks on the river.

Draw four tall trees in a forest.
Draw some plants between the trees.
Draw an animal in the forest.

Evaluation

1 Do the word puzzle.

Down ↓

①

②

④

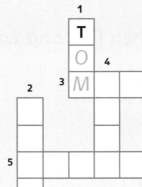

Across →

③

⑤

2 (About Me) **Find and write the questions. Then answer.**

1   are / old / you? / How

How old are you?

I'm

3   swim? / you / Can

_____

_____

5   you / Do / a / have / brother?

_____

_____

2   your / When's / birthday?

_____

_____

4   color? / your / What's / favorite

_____

_____

_____

3 (About Me) **Complete the sentences about this unit.**

1   I can talk about _____ .

2   I can write about _____ .

3   My favorite part is _____ .

4 (Puzzle) **Guess what it is.**

Go to page 93 and circle the answer.

11

1 Look and guess. Then find and write the words.

1

l l r i a r p a e c t

caterpillar

2

t u b y t f l e r

_____

3

s a g r s

_____

4

r e l u t t

_____

5

a i s l n

_____

6

e a g i n u   g i p

_____

7

r e f w o l

_____

8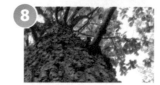

e r e t

_____

9

t r i b a b

_____

10

f e l a

_____

2 Write the words from activity 1 on the lists.

Animals	Plants
caterpillar	_grass_

My picture dictionary Go to page 85: Find and write the new words.

3 **Look and circle the words.**

1. My / **Your** pet is big.
2. His / Their pet is small.
3. His / Her pet is brown.
4. Our / My pet is beautiful.
5. My / Our pet is white.

4 **Look and complete the sentences. Then color the animals.**

~~Her~~ Her His Our	big big ~~small~~ small

1.

   Her pet is _small_ and yellow.

2.

   _____ pet is _____ and gray.

3.

   _____ pet is _____ and brown.

4.

   _____ pet is _____ and orange.

5 Look and circle the questions and answers.

1 (What's that?)
  What are those?

a (It's a snail.)
  They're snails.

2 What's that?
  What are those?

b It's a flower.
  They're flowers.

3 What's that?
  What are those?

c It's a turtle.
  They're turtles.

4 What's that?
  What are those?

d It's a bird.
  They're birds.

5 What's that?
  What are those?

e It's a leaf.
  They're leaves.

6 Look and write the questions and answers.

~~butterflies~~   caterpillar   spider   trees

1 _What are those?_
  They're butterflies.

2 _What's that?_

3 _____

4 _____

Skills: *Writing*

7 **Read the paragraph and write the words.**

> butterflies   leaves   ~~small~~   tree   white

My favorite bug is a caterpillar. Caterpillars are ¹ _small_ . I like black and ² _____ caterpillars. You can see a caterpillar on a ³_____ . The caterpillar eats the green ⁴_____ . Beautiful ⁵_____ come from caterpillars.

8 (About Me) **Answer the questions.**

1 What's your favorite bug?

My favorite bug is _____

2 What color is it?

_____

3 Is it big or small or beautiful?

_____

4 Where can you see it?

_____

9 (About Me) **Write about your favorite bug.**

My favorite bug _____

_____

_____

_____

_____

_____

10 (About Me) **Ask and answer with a friend.**

What's your favorite animal?   My favorite animal is a horse.

Read and match.

1 Not now, Anna.
2 Sorry, Anna. Thank you.
3 Are those ears and a tail?
4 Can we borrow it, please?

Look at activity 11. Answer the questions.

1 What do they see behind the tree?   _Ears and a tail._

2 What animal is behind the tree?   _____

3 What animal does Anna have?   _____

4 What can they do with it?   _____

5 Who is sorry?   _____

13 Look and write the questions and answers. Then check the picture that shows the value: respect and listen to others.

> ~~Can I help?~~   Yes, you can. Thank you.   Can I help?   Not now.

1 *Can I help?*

2

14 Write the words with the same sound in the lists.

> ~~cake~~   ~~tree~~   p<u>ai</u>nt   l<u>ea</u>f   m<u>a</u>ke   j<u>ea</u>ns
> sl<u>ee</u>p   <u>ea</u>t   t<u>ai</u>l   chimpanz<u>ee</u>   tr<u>ai</u>n   sn<u>a</u>ke

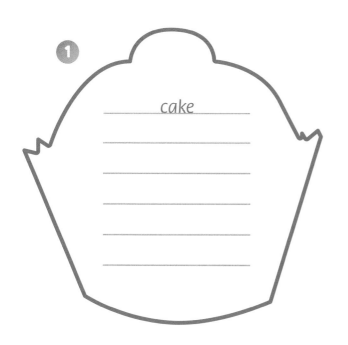

1 *cake*

2 *tree*

What types of habitats are there?

1 **Write the names of the habitats. Then circle the two correct sentences.**

| desert | grassland | ~~rain forest~~ | tundra |

rain forest

It's a hot place.
There are lots of trees and leaves.
Lions live here.

It's a cold place.
There are lots of trees.
Bears live here.

_____

It's a hot place.
Monkeys live here.
There is a lot of grass.

There is little water.
Snakes and spiders live here.
There are lots of fish.

2 **Draw and write about a habitat in your country.**

It's a _____ place. There are lots of _____ . _____ live here.

Evaluation

1 **Find and write the words.**

1 _What's that?_
   It's a flower.

2 _____
   They're leaves.

3 _____
   They're caterpillars.

4 _____
   It's a butterfly.

5 _____
   It's grass.

2 **Look and write the words.**

~~My~~ Your Our Their | ~~turtle~~ fish rabbit snail | ~~small~~ big white green

___My___ ___turtle___   ___ ___   ___ ___   ___ ___
is __small__ .   is _____ .   is _____ .   is _____ .

3 (About Me) **Complete the sentences about this unit.**

1 I can talk about _____ .

2 I can write about _____ .

3 My favorite part is _____ .

4 (Puzzle) **Guess what it is.**

Go to page 93 and circle the answer.

1 Look and number the picture.

1 playground
2 gym
3 science lab
4 sports field
5 cafeteria
6 art room
7 library
8 music room
9 reception
10 classroom

2 Think Look at activity 1. Read the sentences and write the words.

1 You can paint pictures in this room _____art room_____

2 There are desks and chairs in this room. _____

3 You can eat lunch in this room. _____

4 You have a science class in this room. _____

5 You can run, jump, and dance in this room. _____

6 You go here when you visit the school. _____

7 You can play soccer here. _____

8 You can play outside here. _____

9 You can read books here. _____

10 You can sing here. _____

My picture dictionary → Go to page 86: Find and write the new words.

3 **Look and circle the answers.**

We're / (They're) on the sports field.

We're / They're in the art room.

We're / They're in the science lab.

We're / They're in the classroom.

4 **Look and complete the questions and answers.**

1 Where are ___they___ ?   _____ at reception.

2 Where are _____ ?   __We're__ in the library.

3 Where are _____ ?   _____ in the gym.

4 Where are _____ ?   _____ in the music room.

5 Where are _____ ?   _____ on the playground.

5 Read and match.

a They're playing basketball.

b They're playing soccer.

c We're playing basketball.

d We're playing soccer.

6 Look and write the questions and answers.

1 _What are you doing?_   We're _____

2 _____ They're _____

3 _____ _____

4 _____ _____

Skills: *Writing*

7 **Read the text. Circle the answers to the questions.**

My school is (small.) There are six classrooms, a library, and a big playground.

I like the library, but my favorite room is the gym. There are 18 children in my

class. My favorite class is English.

1　Is your school big or small?
2　What rooms and places are in your school?
3　What is your favorite room?
4　How many children are in your class?
5　What is your favorite class?

8 (About Me) **Look at activity 7. Answer the questions.**

1　*My school is* _____

2　_____

3　_____

4　_____

5　_____

9 (About Me) **Write a description of your school.**

My school _____

_____

_____

_____

_____

_____

_____

_____

10 (About Me) **Ask and answer with a friend.**

What's your favorite class?　　　My favorite class is science.

11 Read and write the words.

> Thank you!   pick up   ~~litter~~   Listen!

a

What are they doing?

They're picking up _litter_ . Let's help.

b

Hi, Aunt Pat. Can we help?

Yes, please. Can you _____ this litter?

c

Come on, Lily!

Wait! _____ What's that?

d

Thanks for your help! You can have the radio.

12 Look at activity 11. Write *yes* or *no*.

1 Dad and Aunt Pat are in the gym.   _no_

2 Aunt Pat is picking up litter.   _____

3 The children don't help.   _____

4 Lily is listening to the radio.   _____

5 Aunt Pat wants the radio.   _____

13 Look and check the pictures that show the value: keep your environment clean.

14 Circle the words that sound like *tiger*.

What materials can we recycle?

1 **Look and match.**

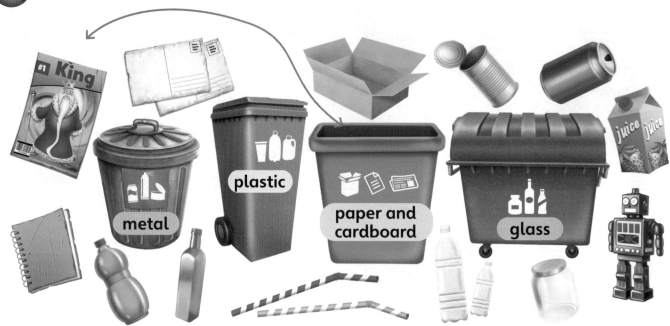

2 **Design two recycling bins for your school.**

Where is it? _____

_____

What can children put in it? _____

_____

Where is it? _____

_____

What can children put in it? _____

_____

Evaluation

 Look and answer the questions.

1   Where are the girls? *They're in the gym.*

2   What are they doing? _____

3   Where are the boys? _____

4   What are they doing? _____

5   Where are the teachers? _____

6   What are they doing? _____

7   Where are we? _____

8   What are we doing? _____

  Complete the sentences about this unit.

1   I can talk about _____ .

2   I can write about _____ .

3   My favorite part is _____ .

  Guess what it is.

Go to page 93 and circle the answer.

Review   Units 1 and 2

1 Look and find the numbers. Answer the questions.

1 Where are they? *They're in the science lab.*

2 What are those? _____

3 What's he doing? _____

4 What are those? _____

5 What are they doing? _____

6 Where are they? _____

7 What's that? _____

8 What's that? _____

2 Think Find 11 months ↓ →. Then answer the question.

```
N O V E M B E R T J S F G M
A C B Z A P Y E J U N E K A
W T A Q Y N A C I L T B O R
B O N J A N U A R Y S R I C
K B U P B T A N G K W U L H
D E C E M B E R X A C A G M
O R O C G M A I O A P R I L
P B Y A U G U S T W B Y J D
```

One month is not in the puzzle. What month is it?

_____

28

3 **Look and write the questions.**

1 _What's her name?_   It's Kate.

2 _____ It's in May.

3 _____ Her favorite color is pink.

4 _Who are they?_   They're my cousins.

5 _____ They're at the park.

6 _____ They're flying a kite.

4 **Look at the photographs in activity 3. Complete the sentences.**

1   _His T-shirt_   is yellow.   2 _____ is pink.

3 _____ are blue.   4 _____ is a plane.

5 **Think Answer the questions.**

> a bird   a butterfly   a caterpillar   a cafeteria
> February   grass   ~~a guinea pig~~   a library

1 These eat leaves. What are they? _A guinea pig_ and _____

2 You can eat here. Where is it? _____

3 You can read books here. Where is it? _____

4 These can fly. What are they? _____ and _____

5 This has 8 letters. What month is it? _____

6 This is a plant. What is it? _____

3 School days

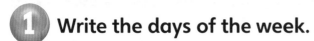

1 Write the days of the week.

	n a d y M o _Monday_	a u s d e T y _____	s d a y d e n W e _____
Sue	 music	pen	microscope
Dan	microscope	sneakers jump rope	brush

Dan   Sue

	y h r d u T s a _____	i a y F d r _____	y r t d S a a u _____	y S n d u a _____
Sue	math	sneakers jump rope	laptop	music
Dan	music	math	soccer ball	laptop

2 Look at activity 1. Write *yes* or *no*.

1 She has math on Thursday. _____ *yes*

2 He has gym on Friday. _____

3 She has art on Monday. _____

4 He has soccer club on Saturday. _____

5 She has computer club on Sunday. _____

3 Look at activity 1. Write the sentences.

1 Monday: _She has music, and he has science._ _____

2 Tuesday: _____

3 Wednesday: _____

4 Thursday: _____

5 Friday: _____

My picture dictionary Go to page 87: Find and write the new words.

4 **Look and follow. Then complete the questions and answers.**

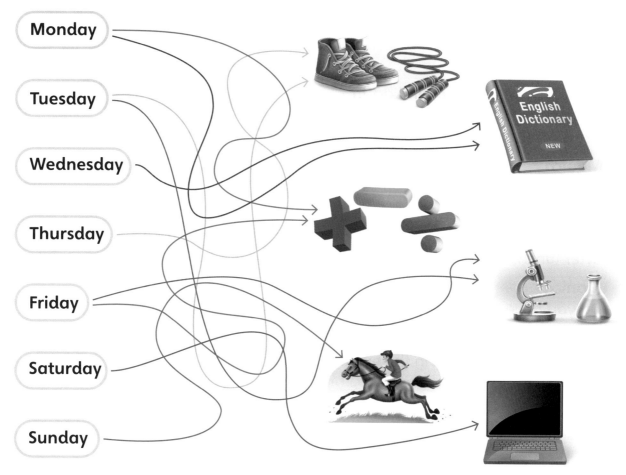

Monday

Tuesday

Wednesday

Thursday

Friday

Saturday

Sunday

1 Do we have gym on Thursday? _____ _Yes, we do._ _____

2 Do we have English on Saturday? _____

3 Do we have math on Monday? _____

4 _____ science on Friday? _____

5 _____ computer club on Sunday? _____

6 _____ horseback riding club on Sunday? _____

5 **Look at activity 4. Complete the sentences.**

1 __We don't have__ math on Thursday.

2 _____ English on Monday and Wednesday.

3 _____ science on Tuesday and Friday.

4 _____ horseback riding club on Thursday.

5 _____ computer club on Saturday.

6 _____ gym on Monday and Friday.

Read and complete Josh's day.

Monica
Which classes do you have on Tuesday?

Josh
We have gym, science, and art in the morning. Gym is before science. Art is after science.

Monica
Which classes do you have in the afternoon?

Josh
We have English and math. We have English after lunch. We have math after English.

Monica
Do you have a club after school?

Josh
Yes, I have soccer club in the evening.

Tuesday

morning
1 _____
2 _____ *science* _____
3 _____
LUNCH
afternoon
4 _____
5 _____
evening
6 _____

7 **Look at activity 6. Write the answers.**

1 Which class does Josh have after gym?

   He has science after gym. _____

2 Which class does Josh have after lunch?

   _____

3 Which class does Josh have before lunch?

   _____

4 Which class does Josh have before math?

   _____

8 **Choose a day from your schedule. Answer the questions.**

1 Which classes do you have in the morning?

   I have _____

2 Which classes do you have in the afternoon?

   _____

3 Do you have a club after school?

   _____

Skills: *Writing*

9 **Read the paragraph and write the words.**

| horseback   club   morning   ~~Saturday~~   music   competitions |

My favorite day of the week is ¹_____Saturday_____ . I have a ²_____

class in the ³_____ . I have photography ⁴_____ in the

afternoon. In the evening. I have a ⁵_____ riding lesson and a dance

competition. I like ⁶_____ .

10 (About Me) **Answer the questions.**

1   What's your favorite day of the week?

My favorite day is _____

2   What do you have in the morning?

_____

3   What do you have in the afternoon?

_____

4   What do you have in the evening?

_____

11 (About Me) **Write about your favorite day.**

My favorite _____

_____

_____

_____

_____

_____

12 (About Me) **Ask and answer with a friend.**

Do you have any clubs this week?

Yes, I have computer club on Thursday.

13 Read and number in order.

a It's very good, Tom.
What do you think, Max?

b We can't take a photograph of the painting.
What can we do now?
I have an idea!

c Is the art gallery open on Saturdays?
Yes, it is.
Come on. Let's go!

d Be careful!
Are you OK, Tom?
Yes, I'm fine. Don't worry.

e OK. Here we are.
Now where's the painting?
Over there!

f What day is it today?
Find this painting.
It's Saturday.
Great! I like art. Let's go to the art gallery.
1

14 Look at activity 13. Answer the questions.

1 Who likes art? _____Tom._____

2 What is open on Saturdays? _____

3 What can't they do? _____

4 What animal is in the painting? _____

5 What does Tom do? _____

15 **Look and check the pictures that show the value: be resourceful.**

16 **Color the words that sound like *goat*. Then answer the question.**

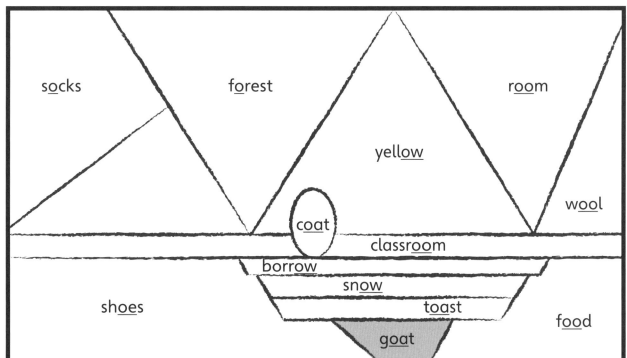

socks   forest   room

yellow

wool

coat

classroom

borrow

snow

toast

shoes   food

goat

What's in the picture? _____

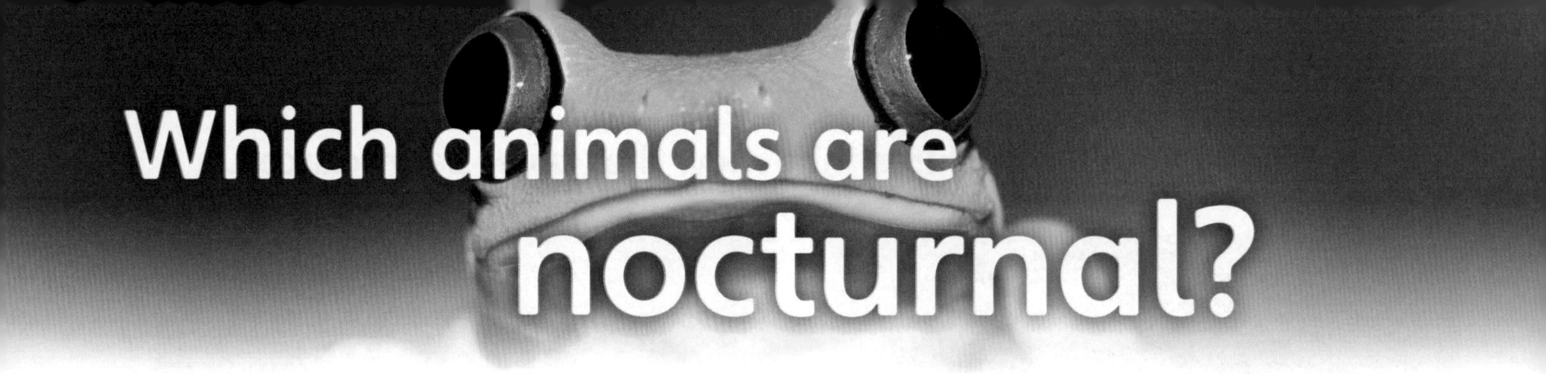

Which animals are nocturnal?

1 **Read and check the sentences that are true for nocturnal animals.**

1 It finds food and eats at night. ✓

2 It likes running and flying in the day. ☐

3 It likes playing in the evening and at night. ☐

4 It sleeps in the morning and afternoon. ☐

2 **Draw and label one animal in each box in the chart.**
Then write sentences about each animal.

	✓ nocturnal	✗ nocturnal
✗ fly	1 	2
✓ fly	3	4

1 _A scorpion is nocturnal. It can't fly._

2 _____

3 _____

4 _____

Evaluation

Emily   Jacob

1 **Write the days of the week in the diary and answer the questions.**

Thursday_____	**Sa**_____
10:00 art	3:00 gym competition
2:00 English test	
6:00 soccer club	
F_____	**S**_____
9:00 gym	10:00 photography club
1:00 science	12:00 lunch with Grandma

1   Do you have art on Friday?   <u>No, we don't.</u>

2   Do you have art on Thursday?   _____

3   Do you have a math test on Thursday?   _____

4   Do you have a gym competition on Saturday?   _____

2 **Look at activity 1. Answer the questions about Emily.**

1   Look at Thursday. What does she have in the morning?   <u>She has art.</u>

2   Look at Thursday. What does she have in the evening?   _____

3   Look at Friday. What does she have in the morning?   _____

4   Look at Friday. What does she have in the afternoon?   _____

5   Look at Sunday. What does she have before lunch?   _____

3 **Complete the sentences about this unit.**

1   I can talk about _____ .

2   I can write about _____ .

3   My favorite part is _____ .

4 **Guess what it is.**

Go to page 93 and circle the answer.

4 My day

1 Look and write the answers.

> brush your teeth · get up · go to bed · ~~go to school~~
> have breakfast · have dinner · have lunch · take a shower

1 _____ go to school _____

2 _____

3 _____

4 _____

5 _____

6 _____

7 _____

8 _____

2 (About Me) Look at activity 1. Write six sentences about your day.

1 I ___ get dressed ___ in the morning.

2 I _____

3 I _____ in the afternoon.

4 I _____ in the evening.

5 _____

6 _____

 My picture dictionary → Go to page 88: Find and write the new words.

3 Read and match.

1   I get dressed at seven o'clock.

2   I go to school at eight o'clock.

3   I eat lunch at twelve o'clock.

4   I go home at three thirty.

5   I eat dinner at seven thirty.

6   I go to bed at nine thirty.

4 Look and complete the sentences.

1   I _____*get up*_____ at _____*seven thirty*_____ .

2   I _____ at _____ .

3   I _____ at _____ .

4   I _____ at _____ .

5   I _____ at _____ .

6   I _____ at _____ .

5 (About Me) Write sentences and draw the times.

1   I *have breakfast* at _____ .

2   I _____ at _____ .

3   I _____ at _____ .

4   I _____ at _____ .

6 Think Read and answer the questions.

Ken: What time do you get up?

Eva: I get up at seven thirty.

Ken: So do I.

Maya: I don't. I get up at seven o'clock.

Maya: What time do you go to bed?

Ken: I go to bed at nine o'clock.

Eva: I don't. I go to bed at eight thirty.

Maya: So do I.

Maya   Eva   Ken

1 Who gets up at seven o'clock?   _____Maya_____

2 Who gets up at seven thirty?   _____ and _____

3 Who goes to bed at eight thirty?   _____ and _____

4 Who goes to bed at nine o'clock?   _____

7 Look and complete the sentences.

1 What time do you have dinner?

I ___have dinner___ at ___seven o'clock___ .

So do I.   I don't.

2 What time do you have breakfast?

I _____ at _____ .

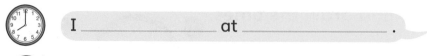

I _____ at _____ .

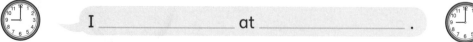

8 About Me Ask and answer with two friends.

I get up at …   So do I.   I don't. I get up at …

Skills: *Writing*

9 **Write a questionnaire about a healthy lifestyle. Then ask a friend.**

~~have breakfast~~   play outside   ~~walk to school~~   ride a bike
~~get up~~   brush your teeth   watch TV   play sports
play computer games   drink orange juice

Yes / No

1 Do you have breakfast every day? _____

2 Do you walk to school in the morning? _____

3 Do you like getting up early? _____

4 _____

5 _____

6 _____

7 _____

8 _____

9 _____

10 _____

10   **Ask and answer with a friend.**

Do you have a healthy lifestyle?   Yes, I do. I walk to school every day.

11 Read and match.

> 1 I can do the race! 2 Thanks! Swimming is fun!
> 3 The first prize is a watch! 4 And the winner is ... Lucas!

12 Look at activity 11. Circle the answers.

1 Lucas does _____ .
a a swimming club   **b a swimming race**   c the first prize

2 Lucas thinks swimming is _____ .
a fun   b great   c nice

3 Lucas wins _____ .
a a present   b a test   c a prize

4 The prize is _____ .
a a watch   b a race   c swimming lessons

13 Check the activities that show the value: exercise.

1 do a bike race ✓

2 go to baseball club

3 take a math test

4 play in a tennis competition

5 go to bed early

6 go roller-skating

7 take a shower

8 play sports after school

14 Circle the words that sound like *blue*.

START!

blue	equals	snow	jump	toast	sausage
turn	June	run	goat	excuse	plus
yellow	mouth	shoots	chew	duck	room

FINISH!

What time is it around the world?

1 **Look and answer the questions.**

1 What time is it in Buenos Aires?

It's ___eight o'clock___ in the morning.

2 What time is it in London?

It's _____ in the afternoon.

3 What time is it in Dubai?

It's _____.

4 What time is it in Shanghai?

It's _____.

2 **Draw a picture and write sentences.**

1 I _____ at eight o'clock in the morning.

2 I _____
_____.

3 I _____
_____.

4 I _____
_____.

Evaluation

1 **Look and complete the questions and answers.**

1 What time do you get up?

I get up at six thirty.

2 What time do you get dressed?

_____

3 _____

I go to school at eight o'clock.

4 _____

I have dinner at half past seven.

5 What time do you brush your teeth?

_____

6 _____

I go to bed at nine o'clock.

2 (About Me) **Look at activity 1. Write sentences. Start with *So do I* or *I don't*.**

1 *So do I. I get up at six thirty.* _____

2 _____

3 _____

4 _____

5 _____

6 _____

3 (About Me) **Complete the sentences about this unit.**

1 I can talk about _____ .

2 I can write about _____ .

3 My favorite part is _____ .

4 Puzzle **Guess what it is.**

Go to page 93 and circle the answer.

45

Review Units 3 and 4

1 **Look and complete the sentences about my day.**

> after lunch   after school   at four o'clock
> at nine o'clock.   at six thirty   at ten o'clock

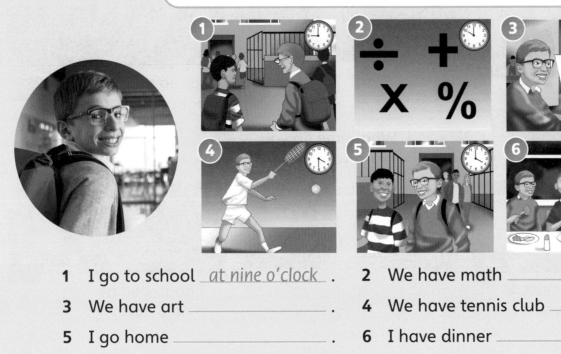

1 I go to school _at nine o'clock_ .

2 We have math _____ .

3 We have art _____ .

4 We have tennis club _____ .

5 I go home _____ .

6 I have dinner _____ .

2 (About Me) **Write questions and answers.**

> ~~get up~~   go to bed   have breakfast | ~~on Monday~~   on Saturday   on Sunday

1 _What time do you get up on Monday?_
   I get up _____

2 _____
   _____

3 _____
   _____

4 _____
   _____

3 Find the words ↓ →. Use the words to complete the verbs.

1

get _dressed_

2

take a _____

B	H	F	D	T	E	E	T	H
R	W	V	I	P	K	E	X	M
E	L	U	N	C	H	L	U	S
A	O	Y	N	C	G	B	A	C
K	D	R	E	S	S	E	D	H
F	M	E	R	B	O	D	C	O
A	Z	R	W	E	G	H	H	O
S	H	O	W	E	R	Q	R	L
T	X	L	B	A	U	P	C	Z

3

brush your _____

4

have _____

5

go to _____

6

have _____

7

have _____

8

go to _____

4 **Answer the questions.**

1 What day starts with the letter *M*? _____ _Monday_ _____

2 What day has nine letters? _____

3 What day comes after Thursday? _____

4 What day comes before Sunday? _____

5 What day has the letter *H* in it? _____

6 What day sounds like M<u>o</u>nday? _____

7 Put these letters in order: YADSUTE. _____

5 Home time

1 Look and match.

a listen to music

b eat a sandwich

c do the dishes

d read a book

e drink juice

f make a cake

g watch TV

h wash the car

2 Look at activity 1. Complete the sentences.

1 Look at picture 1.   He's _____reading a book_____ .

2 Look at picture 2.   He's _____ .

3 Look at picture 4.   She's _____ .

4 Look at picture 6.   She's _____ .

5 Look at picture 7.   He's _____ .

3 (About Me) Answer the questions.

1 Do you like listening to music? _____

2 Do you like playing on the computer? _____

3 Do you like doing homework? _____

My picture dictionary ➡ Go to page 89: Find and write the new words.

Read and match.

1   I love making cakes.

2   My mom likes listening to music.

3   My sister enjoys doing homework.

4   My brother doesn't enjoy playing this game on the computer.

5   My dad doesn't like doing the dishes.

 Look and complete the sentences.

| like   love   doesn't enjoy   ~~doesn't like~~ | ~~drink~~   read   wash   watch |

He _doesn't like drinking_ juice.

She _____ books.

He _____ TV.

She _____ the car.

(About Me) Write about your friend.

Name: _____

1   _____ loves _____ .

2   _____ likes _____ .

3   _____ doesn't enjoy _____ .

7 Look and complete the questions. Then circle the answers.

1 Does he like _____ *reading books* _____ ? (Yes, he does.) / No, he doesn't.

2 Does she enjoy _____ ? Yes, she does. / No, she doesn't.

3 Does she like _____ ? Yes, she does. / No, she doesn't.

4 Does he like _____ ? Yes, he does. / No, he doesn't.

5 Does he enjoy _____ ? Yes, he does. / No, he doesn't.

6 Does she like _____ ? Yes, she does. / No, she doesn't.

8 (Think) Look and complete the questions and answers. Then draw.

Does she enjoy ___ *making* ___ a cake?

No, ___ *she doesn't* ___ .

_____ enjoy_____ TV?

No, _____ .

_____ love _____
on the computer?

Yes, _____ .

_____ like _____
homework?

Yes, _____ .

Skills: *Writing*

9 **Read the paragraph and write the words.**

> love eating   enjoy cleaning   don't like doing   enjoy washing   ~~like making~~

I'm helpful at home. In the morning, I ¹ *like making* cakes, and

I ² _____ them! I ³ _____ my bedroom, too. In the

afternoon, I'm helpful. I ⁴ _____ the dog or the car.

After dinner, I'm not helpful. I ⁵ _____ the dishes!

10 (About Me) **Answer the questions.**

1 What do you enjoy cleaning?

  I enjoy _____

2 What do you like washing?

  _____

3 What do you like making?

  _____

4 What do you love doing?

  _____

5 What don't you like doing?

  _____

11 (About Me) **Write about being helpful at home.**

  I'm helpful at home. I like _____

  _____

  _____

  _____

  _____

12 (About Me) **Ask and answer with a friend.**

Do you like cleaning your bedroom?   Yes, I do.

13 Read and write the words.

> need   Watch out   so sorry   ~~likes making~~

a My Aunt Pat _likes making_ cakes.

Find a chocolate cake.

Great! Let's go to her house!

b What do we _____ ?

Eggs, milk, chocolate …

c _____ , Lucas!

Oh, no!

d Oh, dear! I'm _____ .

Me, too!

14 Look at activity 13. Answer the questions.

1 Where are the children going?   _Aunt Pat's house._

2 Does Aunt Pat like making cakes?   _____

3 What do they need to make the cake? _____

4 What does Lucas drop?   _____

5 Who's sorry?   _____

15 Look and check the picture that shows the value: show forgiveness.

16 Color the words that sound like *teeth*. Then answer the question.

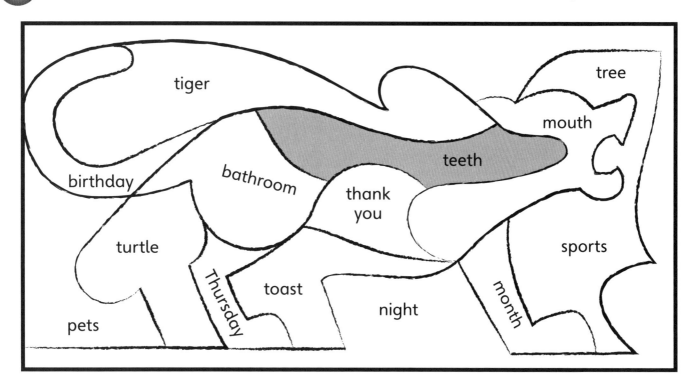

What's this animal? _____

Where do people live?

1 Find the words and write under the pictures.

~~wont~~   llivgea   ytic   ouidecyrtns

_____

_____

_____

<u>town</u>

2 Look and complete the sentences.

café   houses   riding   stores   supermarket   town   ~~village~~   walking

In the ¹_____*village*_____ there
is a small ²_____ . There
are two ³_____ . People
like ⁴_____ their bikes there.

In the ⁵_____ , there are a lot
of ⁶_____ and some stores.
You can buy food at the
⁷_____ . A lot of people
are ⁸_____ in the street.

Evaluation

1 Read and match. Then answer the questions.

Tom

1 read a book

2 do the dishes

3 do homework

4 listen to music

5 make a cake

6 drink juice

Cara

1 Does she like reading a book? _Yes, she does._

2 Does she love doing the dishes? _____

3 Does he like doing homework? _____

4 Does he enjoy drinking juice? _____

2 Look at activity 1. Complete the sentences.

1 Tom enjoys _doing homework_ .

2 Tom loves _____ , but he doesn't like _____ .

3 Cara loves _____ .

4 Cara doesn't enjoy _____ , but she likes _____ .

3 (About Me) Complete the sentences about this unit.

1 I can talk about _____ .

2 I can write about _____ .

3 My favorite part is _____ .

4 Puzzle Guess what it is.

Go to page 93 and circle the answer.

6 Hobbies

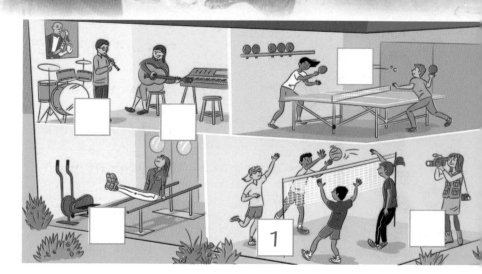

1 **Look and number the picture.**

1 play volleyball
2 make movies
3 do gymnastics
4 play the guitar
5 play Ping-Pong
6 play the recorder

2 **Look and write the words.**

| make   do   ~~play~~   play | models   ~~badminton~~   the piano   karate |

 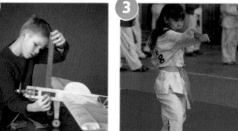 

1 ___play___
___badminton___

2 _____ _____

3 _____ _____

4 _____ _____

3 **Write the words from activities 1 and 2 on the lists.**

Crafts	Music	Sports
make movies	_____	_____
_____	_____	_____
	_____	_____
		_____

| **My picture dictionary** ➡ Go to page 90: Find and write the new words. |

Look and follow. Then write *true* or *false*.

Dan   Anna   Claire   Jamie   May

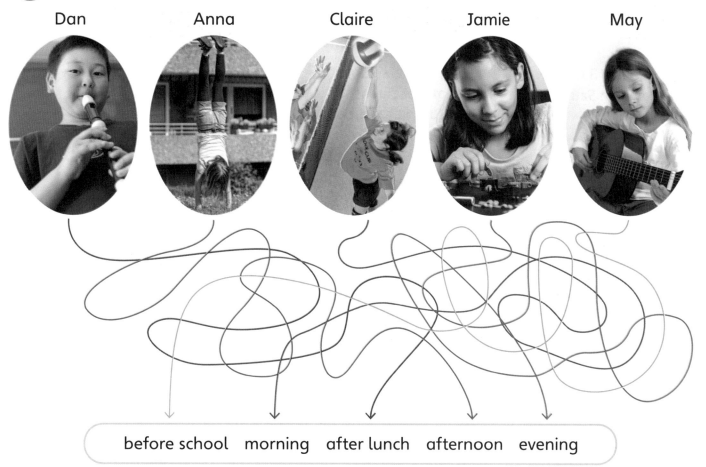

before school   morning   after lunch   afternoon   evening

1 Dan plays the recorder before school.   *false*

2 Anna does gymnastics in the afternoon.   _____

3 Claire plays volleyball in the evening.   _____

4 Jamie makes models in the morning.   _____

5 May plays the guitar before school.   _____

 Look at activity 4. Complete the sentences.

1 Dan _doesn't play the recorder_ before school.

2 Anna _____ in the afternoon.

3 Claire _____ in the evening.

4 Jamie _____ in the morning.

5 May _____ before school.

6 Look and read. Then answer the questions.

Hi, Jack. Baseball game on Saturday morning.

Jack, remember model club is Tuesday afternoon. Ben

Hello, Jack. Don't forget gymnastics club Tuesday morning before school. Mom

Ella, see you Thursday evening for your piano lesson.

Hi, Ella. Don't forget movie club is Friday evening! Amy

Ella. Remember karate club Sunday morning. Dad

1	Does Jack play baseball on Saturdays?	*Yes, he does.*
2	Does Ella play piano in the afternoon?	
3	Does Jack make models in the evening?	
4	Does Ella make movies on Sundays?	
5	Does Jack do gymnastics before school?	
6	Does Ella do karate on Sundays?	

7 Write questions about Jack and Ella.

do gymnastics   make movies   make models
~~play the guitar~~   play the piano   play volleyball

1 ___Does___ Jack _play the guitar_ on Saturdays? No, he doesn't.

2 _____ Ella _____ on Thursdays? Yes, she does.

3 _____ Jack _____ on Tuesdays? Yes, he does.

4 _____ Ella _____ in the evening? Yes, she does.

5 _____ Jack _____ in the morning? Yes, he does.

6 _____ Ella _____ on Sundays? No, she doesn't.

Skills: *Writing*

8 **Read the paragraph and write the words.**

after school   competitions   drink   hungry   ~~swimming~~   afternoon

My favorite sport is ¹___swimming___ . I swim every Saturday and Sunday

²_____ . Sometimes there are ³_____ . I'm always

⁴_____ after swimming! I eat a sandwich and ⁵_____

a glass of milk. I enjoy playing tennis, too. We play ⁶_____ on Friday.

9 (About Me) **Answer the questions.**

1 What is your favorite sport?

 My favorite sport is _____

2 When do you do it?

 _____

3 Are there any competitions?

 _____

4 What do you eat and drink after playing sports?

 _____

10 (About Me) **Write about your favorite sport.**

 My favorite sport _____

 _____

 _____

 _____

 _____

 _____

11 (About Me) **Ask and answer with a friend.**

What's your favorite sport?   My favorite sport is horseback riding.

12 Read and number in order.

13 Look at activity 12. Circle the answers.

1 Who plays in a band?
   a Tom's cousin   **b** Lily's cousin *(circled)*   **c** Lily

2 Who wants to play guitar with Kim?
   a Lily   **b** Anna   **c** Tom

3 What can't Lucas do?
   a play in a band   **b** find a guitar   **c** play the guitar

4 What is fun for Lucas?
   a watching Kim   **b** trying new things   **c** playing in a band

5 What does Kim want Lucas to do every day?
   a practice the guitar   **b** play in Kim's band   **c** try new things

14 **Look and check the pictures that show the value: try new things.**

15 **Circle the words that sound like *shark*.**

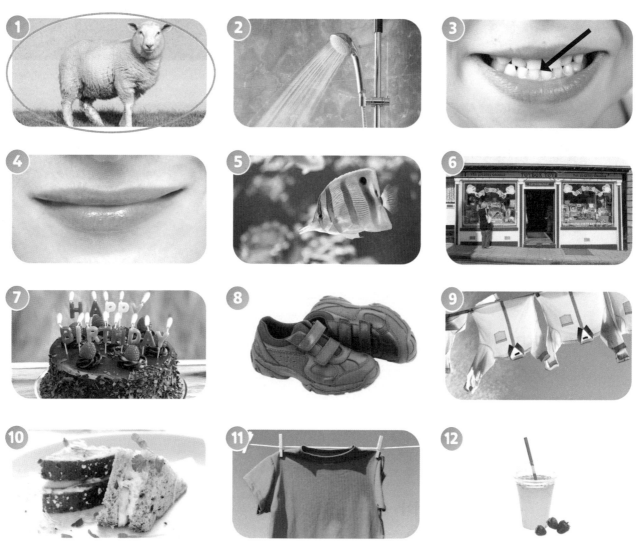

What type of musical instrument is it?

1 Look and guess. Then find and write the words.

girstn   srabs   sserciupon   ~~wwddinoo~~

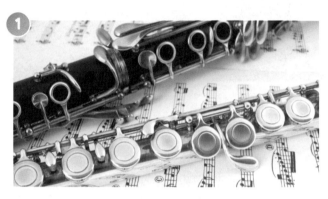

woodwind

2 Complete the sentences.

1 The drum _____ is a percussion instrument _____.

2 The guitar _____.

3 The piano _____.

4 The recorder _____.

3 Ask and answer with a friend.

What instrument do you like?   I like the piano!

Evaluation

1 Look and complete the Venn diagram. Then answer the questions.

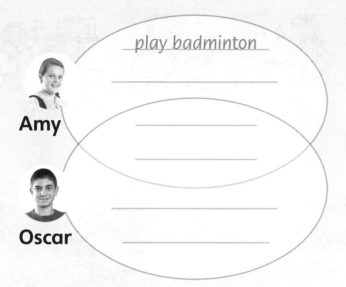

play badminton

Amy

Oscar

Day	Amy	Oscar
Monday morning		
Tuesday after school		
Thursday afternoon		
Friday evening		

1 Does Amy play the piano on Tuesdays? *Yes, she does.*

2 Does Oscar play the piano on Tuesdays? _____

3 Does Amy do karate on Fridays? _____

4 Does Oscar do karate on Tuesdays? _____

2 Look at activity 1. Complete the sentences about Oscar.

1 *He doesn't play* Ping-Pong after school.

2 _____ gymnastics on Wednesdays.

3 _____ karate in the morning.

4 _____ the piano on Fridays.

3 (About Me) Complete the sentences about this unit.

1 I can talk about _____ .

2 I can write about _____ .

3 My favorite part is _____ .

4 (Puzzle) Guess what it is.

Go to page 93 and circle the answer.

63

Review Units 5 and 6

1 Look and answer the questions.

Jade	☹	☺	☺	☺
Ben	☺	☹	☹	☺

1 Does Ben enjoy playing Ping-Pong? <u>Yes, he does.</u>

2 Does Jade like playing Ping-Pong? _____

3 Does Ben like reading? _____

4 Does Jade love listening to music? _____

5 Does Ben enjoy playing the guitar? _____

6 Does Jade love playing the guitar? _____

Ben   Jade

2 Look at activity 1. Complete the sentences.

1 Jade loves <u>listening to music</u> , but she doesn't like _____ .

2 Ben enjoys _____ , but he doesn't like _____ .

3 Jade likes _____ , but she loves _____ .

4 Ben loves _____ , but he doesn't like _____ .

3 (About Me) Answer the questions.

1 Do you like playing Ping-Pong?

_____

2 Do you like playing the guitar?

_____

3 Do you like making lunch?

_____

4 Do you like washing clothes?

_____

4 Think **Look and write the verbs on the lists.**

do

1 *do your homework*

2 _____

3 _____

make

4 _____

5 _____

6 _____

play

7 _____

8 _____

9 _____

5 About Me **Look at activity 4. Write sentences.**

1 I _____ in the afternoon.

2 I _____ on Saturdays.

3 I like _____ , but _____ .

4 I enjoy _____ , but _____ .

1 Look and do the word puzzle.

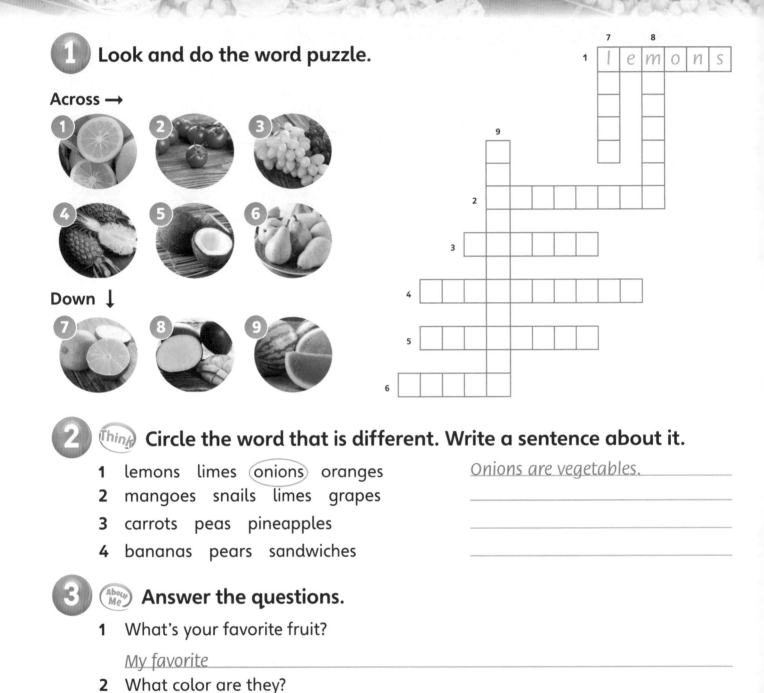

Across →

1 2 3

4 5 6

Down ↓

7 8 9

	7	8			
1	l	e	m	o	n	s

2 Think Circle the word that is different. Write a sentence about it.

1 lemons limes (onions) oranges   *Onions are vegetables.*

2 mangoes snails limes grapes

3 carrots peas pineapples

4 bananas pears sandwiches

3 About Me Answer the questions.

1 What's your favorite fruit?

My favorite

2 What color are they?

3 Are they big or small?

My picture dictionary Go to page 91 : Find and write the new words.

Read and circle the correct pictures.

1 There are lots of pineapples.

a    b    c

2 There are some onions.

a    b    c

3 There aren't any tomatoes.

a    b    c

4 There are lots of mangoes.

a    b    c

5 **Look and complete the sentences with *lots of*, *some*, or *not any*.**

1 There _____*aren't any*_____ onions.

2 There _____ vegetables.

3 There _____ bananas.

4 There _____ tomatoes.

5 There _____ carrots.

6 Look and check *yes* or *no*.

	Yes, there are.	No, there aren't.
1 Are there any apples?	☐	✓
2 Are there any carrots?	☐	☐
3 Are there any mangoes?	☐	☐
4 Are there any beans?	☐	☐
5 Are there any watermelons?	☐	☐

7 Look at activity 6. Complete the questions and answers.

1 _____Are there any_____ grapes? _____Yes, there are._____

2 _____ coconuts? _____

3 _____ lemons? _____

4 _____ pineapples? _____

5 _____ oranges? _____

Skills: *Writing*

8 **Read the paragraph and write the words.**

> any   aren't   ~~favorite~~   juice   like   some

My ¹___favorite___ smoothie is Tropical Yum. I like orange ²_____ .
It's in my favorite smoothie. Bananas are my favorite fruit. There are
³_____ bananas in my smoothie. There aren't ⁴_____ limes.
I don't ⁵_____ them. They ⁶_____ sweet.

9 (About Me) **Answer the questions.**

1   What's your favorite smoothie? Can you think of a name for it?
    _My favorite smoothie is_____

2   Which juice do you like? Is it in your smoothie?
    _____

3   Make a list of the fruit in your smoothie.
    _____

4   What fruit don't you like in your smoothie?
    _____

10 (About Me) **Write about your favorite smoothie.**

_My favorite smoothie_____
_____
_____
_____
_____
_____

11 (About Me) **Ask and answer with a friend.**

What's your favorite smoothie?   My favorite smoothie is …

12 Read and write the words.

are   has   ~~lots of~~   red one   don't have

a

There are __lots of__ purses.

We _____ any money.

b

There _____ lots of old clothes in here.

Great! Let's look for a purse!

c

Yes! Look!

She _____ two purses!

d

Which purse do you want?

The _____ .

13 Look at activity 12. Circle the answers.

1   They're looking for a _____ .
   a purse   **b** guitar   **c** hat

2   They don't have any _____ .
   a shoes   **b** old clothes   **c** money

3   There are lots of _____ .
   a new clothes   **b** big clothes   **c** old clothes

4   Anna has _____ .
   a an old purse   **b** two purses   **c** two red purses

5   Lily wants the _____ .
   a blue purse   **b** red purse   **c** new purse

14 **Look and check the pictures that show the value: reuse old things.**

15 **Draw the shapes around the words with the same sound.**

▭ = sh ⬭ = ch

What parts of plants can we eat?

1 **Look and guess. Then find and write the words.**

~~pragse~~ nabasan sepa insono torcars

grapes

_____

_____

_____

_____

2 **Look at activity 1. Read and complete the sentences.**

1 They're seeds. They're small. They're green. They're _____peas_____ .

2 They're roots. They're orange. Rabbits like eating them. They're _____ .

3 They're purple fruit. We can't buy one. We buy lots of them. They're _____ .

4 They're stems. They're long. We don't eat them for breakfast. They're _____ .

5 They're yellow fruit. Monkeys enjoy eating them. They're _____ .

Evaluation

  1 **Think** **Color the fruits and vegetables. Then answer the questions.**

1 Are there any apples? _Yes, there are._

2 Are there any grapes? _____

3 Are there any pears? _____

4 Are there any watermelons? _____

5 Are there any carrots? _____

6 Are there any pineapples? _____

2 **About Me** **Write about your classroom.**

> pencils   desks   flowers   ~~books~~   rabbits   windows

1 There are lots of ___books___ .

2 There are some _____ .

3 There aren't any _____ .

4 _____

5 _____ .

6 _____

3 **About Me** **Complete the sentences about this unit.**

1 I can talk about _____ .

2 I can write about _____ .

3 My favorite part is _____ .

4 **Puzzle** **Guess what it is.**

> Go to page 93 and circle the answer.

8 At the beach

1 Look and write the words. Then color the picture.

1 Color the __sun__ yellow.

2 Next to the towel is a _____ . Color it pink.

3 On the towel are some red and white _____ .

4 Can you see some _____ ? Color them blue.

2 Find and circle. Then match and write the words.

friesswimsuitoceantowelsandburger

fries

My picture dictionary Go to page 92: Find and write the new words.

3 (Think) **Look and write the words.**

hers   his   mine   ours   ~~theirs~~   yours

1 Which umbrella is ___theirs___ ? The red one.

2 Which umbrella is _____ ? The purple one.

3 Which sock is _____ ? The white one.

4 Which sock is _____ ? The yellow one.

5 Which hat is _____ ?

6 The green one's _____ .

4 **Look and answer the questions.**

1 Which shell is his?   _The yellow one's his._

2 Which shell is hers?   _____

3 Which towel is theirs?   _____

4 Which towel is ours?   _____

5 Which rabbit is mine?   _____

5 **Look and circle the words.**

Whose jacket is **that** / **this**?
It's / **They're** Ana's.

Whose shoes are **these** / **those**?
It's / **They're** theirs.

Whose bags are **these** / **those**?
It's / **They're** yours.

Whose sunglasses are **these** / **those**?
It's / **They're** mine.

Whose house is **this** / **that**?
It's / **They're** ours.

6 **Look and complete the questions and answers.**

____Whose____ hat ____is this____ ?

____It's____ his.

_____ bike _____ ?

_____ Tim's.

_____ paintings _____ ?

_____ mine.

_____ pencils _____ ?

_____ theirs.

Skills: *Writing*

7 **Read the postcard and answer the questions.**

1 Where is Dylan? _At the beach._
2 What does he like doing in the morning?
_____
3 Who does he enjoy playing with?
_____
4 What does he do in the afternoon?
_____
5 What does he eat for lunch?
_____

> Dear Renata,
>   We are having a lovely vacation. We're at the beach.
>   I like flying my kite in the morning. I enjoy playing with my sister. In the afternoon, I swim in the ocean. It's great. There are lots of people swimming in the ocean. But there aren't any sharks. ☺
>   At lunchtime we go to the café. I eat sausages and fries.
>   See you soon,
>   Dylan

8 (About Me) **Imagine you're on vacation. Answer the questions.**

1 Where are you?   _I'm_ _____
2 Who is on holiday with you?
_____
3 What do you do in the morning?
_____
4 What do you do in the afternoon?
_____
5 What do you eat?
_____

9 (About Me) **Write a postcard to a friend.**

Dear _____
I'm having a _____
_____
_____
_____

10 (About Me) **Ask and answer with a friend.**

What do you do on vacation?   I swim in the ocean.

11 Read and match.

1 Hi. Do you have my seven things?	**2** Good idea. Let's ask my dad.
3 We hope you enjoy it!	**4** Thank you, Mr. Lin.

a How should we get to the movie theater?

Let's go by car.

___2___

b _____

Wait a minute! Whose car is that?

It's Aunt Pat's.

c _____

Aunt Pat!

d Welcome to our show!

_____

12 Look at activity 11. Circle the answers.

1 Where do they go?
   a to the supermarket   **b** to the school   **c** to the movie theater

2 How do they get there?
   a by bike   **b** by car   **c** by bus

3 How many things do they have?
   a three   **b** five   **c** seven

4 Whose things are they?
   a Lily's   **b** Aunt Pat's   **c** Mr. Lin's

5 What are the things for?
   a family and friends   **b** Anna   **c** a show

13 **Look and write the answers. Then check the picture that shows the value: appreciate your family and friends.**

Thank you!   ~~Dinner is ready!~~   Five minutes, Mom!   You're a great dad!

14 **Circle the words that sound like *dolphin*.**

Are sea animals symmetrical?

1 **Look and write the words.**

jellyfish   octopus   crab   ~~shell~~   sea horse   starfish

shell

2 **Look at activity 1. Write about the sea animals.**

1   *This shell is small. In this picture, the shell is symmetrical.*

2   _____

3   _____

4   _____

5   _____

6   _____

Evaluation

1 Look and do the word puzzle.

Across

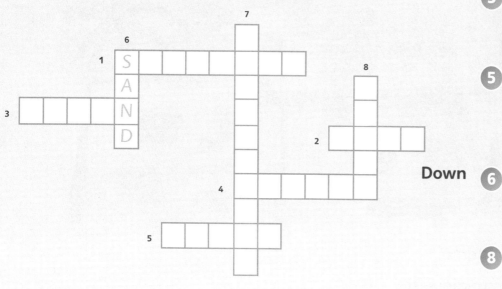

Down

(Crossword grid)

1 **S** A N D

3

5

7

2

4

6

8

2 Look and circle the answers.

1 Whose backpack is this? It's **hers** / **his**.

2 Whose ball is this? It's **his** / **hers**.

3 Which hat is his? **It's the white one.** / **It's the red one.**

4 Which jacket is hers? **It's the green one.** / **It's the blue one.**

3 (About Me) Complete the sentences about this unit.

1 I can talk about _____.

2 I can write about _____.

3 My favorite part is _____.

4 (Puzzle) Guess what it is.

Go to page 93 and circle the answer.

Review Units 7 and 8

1 Look and answer the questions.

1	Are there any shorts?	_Yes, there are._
2	Are there any sunglasses?	
3	Are there any shells?	
4	Is there a swimsuit?	
5	Is there a towel?	
6	Are there any pineapples?	
7	Are there any lemons?	
8	Is there a watermelon?	
9	Are there any onions?	
10	Are there any coconuts?	

2 Look and match. Complete the sentences with *some*, *lots of*, or *not any*.

1 _There are some_ tomatoes.
2 _____ pears.
3 _____ lemons.
4 _____ shells.
5 _____ grapes.
6 _____ fries.

3 **Look and circle the words.**

1 Whose pineapple is **this** / **that**?

It's / **They're** yours.

2 Whose onions are **these** / **those**?

It's / **They're** yours.

3 Whose limes are **these** / **those**?

It's / **They're** mine.

4 Whose shell is **this** / **that**?

It's / **They're** mine.

4 **Think** **Look and circle the words. Then answer the questions.**

1 Which camera is **hers** / **yours**?

The small one's mine.

2 Which kite is **his** / **yours**?

_____

3 Which pencil case is **his** / **ours**?

_____

4 Which towel is **his** / **theirs**?

_____

5 Which bag is **hers** / **his**?

_____

Welcome

Lucas ~~Anna~~ Max Tom Lily

Anna

March December ~~January~~ August April October
June November May February July September

J a n u a r y	**F** _ _ _ _ _ _ _	**M** _ _ _ _ _
A _ _ _ _ _	**M** _ _	**J** _ _ _ _
J _ _ _	**A** _ _ _ _ _	**S** _ _ _ _ _ _ _ _
O _ _ _ _ _ _	**N** _ _ _ _ _ _ _	**D** _ _ _ _ _ _ _

① In the yard

snail   guinea pig   caterpillar   turtle   ~~butterfly~~
tree   flower   grass   rabbit   leaf

butterfly

reception   library   sports field   classroom   gym   music room
cafeteria   ~~art room~~   playground   science lab

art room

3 School days

Saturday   Tuesday   ~~Monday~~   Thursday
Sunday   Wednesday   Friday

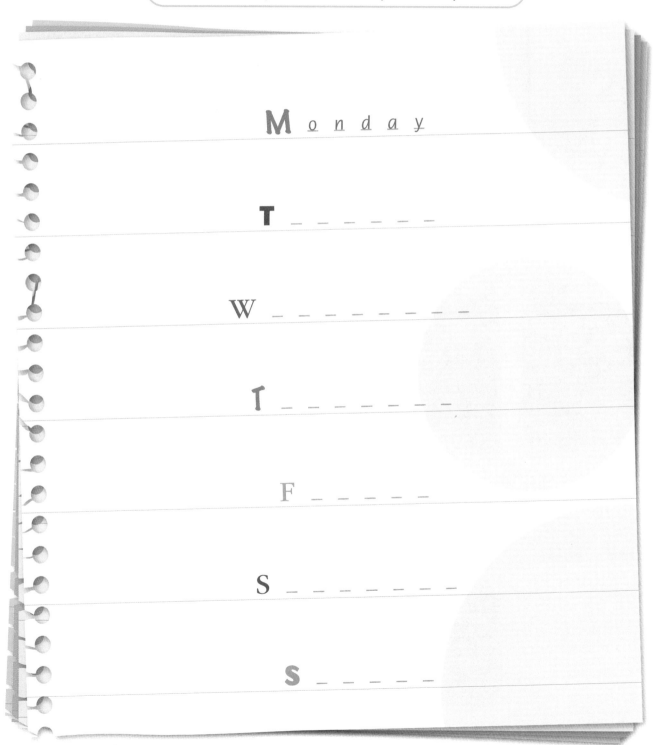

M o n d a y

T _ _ _ _ _ _

W _ _ _ _ _ _ _ _

T _ _ _ _ _ _ _

F _ _ _ _ _

S _ _ _ _ _ _ _

S _ _ _ _ _

4 My day

go to school   get up   take a shower   have breakfast   get dressed
have lunch   go home   have dinner   ~~brush your teeth~~   go to bed

brush your teeth

5 Home time

do homework   watch TV   ~~do the dishes~~   listen to music   wash the car
play on the computer   drink juice   make a cake   read a book   eat a sandwich

do the dishes

6 Hobbies

play the recorder   play Ping-Pong   do karate   play badminton   make models
play the guitar   make movies   play the piano   ~~do gymnastics~~   play volleyball

do gymnastics

7 At the market

onions ~~coconuts~~ watermelons mangoes pineapples
tomatoes limes pears lemons grapes

coconuts _____ _____ _____ _____

_____ _____ _____ _____

_____ _____

swimsuit   fries   shells   sun   ~~burger~~   sunglasses   sand   towel   ocean   shorts

burger

_____

_____

_____

_____

_____

_____

_____

_____

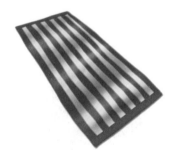

_____

My puzzle

1 **Find the words ↓ →. Use the colored letters to answer the question.**

P	G	L	I	B	R	A	R	Y	A	R	C	U	B
I	Q	E	R	T	G	Y	J	K	E	L	P	V	E
N	L	A	B	U	T	T	E	R	F	L	Y	U	V
E	B	Z	M	S	W	L	H	B	G	T	D	A	M
A	M	N	F	O	T	D	W	B	I	I	S	O	A
P	G	O	A	O	S	H	O	W	E	R	H	X	T
P	A	A	N	M	G	I	R	C	M	Q	E	Z	H
I	S	G	N	H	K	L	U	Y	O	O	L	P	M
E	M	U	A	N	T	U	E	R	N	S	L	L	Y
X	V	I	E	B	G	H	Y	O	P	W	F	R	Y
D	O	T	H	E	D	I	S	H	E	S	O	K	R
J	K	A	S	K	V	B	Y	U	W	E	T	R	E
M	I	R	W	T	E	C	J	F	H	A	N	N	A

Q: What are two things people can't eat before breakfast?

A: _ _ _ _ _ _ and _ _ _ _ _ _ _!

Story fun

1 Match the objects to the words. Then match the words to the story units they come from.

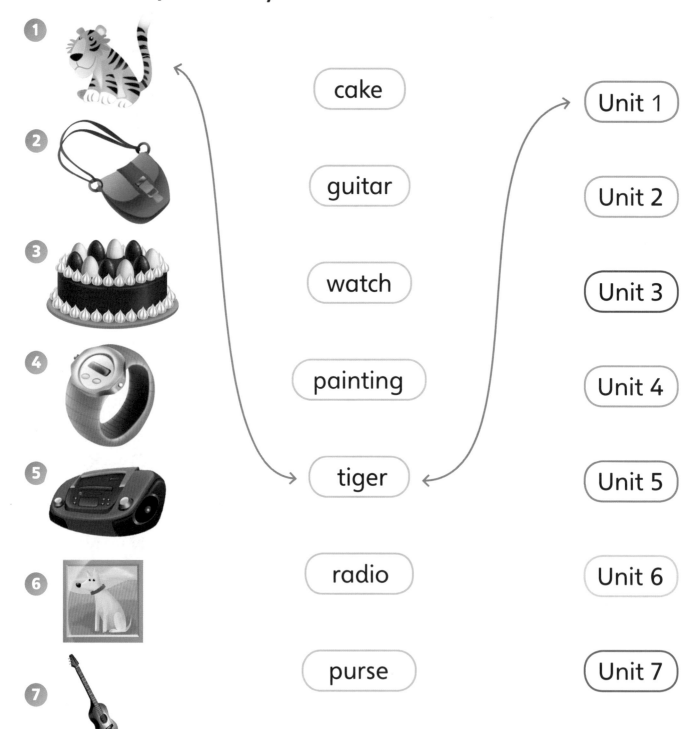

cake — Unit 1

guitar — Unit 2

watch — Unit 3

painting — Unit 4

tiger — Unit 5

radio — Unit 6

purse — Unit 7

1 Write the numbers in the box of the objects in Aunt Pat's show.